NEWT GINGRICH'S BEDTIME STORIES FOR ORPHANS

as overheard by

Cathy Crimmins

and

Tom Maeder

DOVE
BOOKS

ISBN 0-7871-0578-3

Printed in the United States of America

Dove Books
301 North Cañon Drive
Beverly Hills, CA 90210

Distributed by Penguin USA

Text design and layout by Michele Lanci-Altomare
Jacket design and illustration by Rick Penn-Kraus
Line art illustrations by Wesla Weller

10 9 8 7 6 5 4 3 2

TABLE OF CONTENTS

April 1, 2002

Dear Fellow Americans,

Ever since President Gingrich was elected, we've been following him around during his visits to the state orphanages. The man is just wonderful with children. Time after time, we've witnessed touching scenes as he tells the little tykes bedtime stories and tucks them into bed. "Uncle Newt makes me feel like I have a real daddy, whatever that is!" said one young boy, summing up the excitement these homeless waifs feel during a presidential visit.

Many people have written to us, saying: "It's not fair that you have to be an orphan to hear the President's stories." We agree. These are tales that bear repeating. So, we're offering the transcripts of our taped orphanage story sessions here for everybody to read, along with some of the comments from the parentless boys and girls who have touched our hearts.

As our hero Father Flanagan of Boys Town always said, "There is no such thing as a bad boy." In President Gingrich's book, and in this book, there is no such thing as a bad orphan or a bad tale. Enjoy!

Cathy Crimmins and Tom Maeder

Uncle Newt's visits to orphanages are always a cause for special celebration. The work day in the orphanage industries is cut short so that the boys and girls can display their drill team exercises on the parade ground. Then it's prayer session and dinner with an extra helping of gruel, followed by a half-hour discussion of the principles of self-government.

Later, the orphans change into their pajamas, say the Pledge of Allegiance, and sing the national anthem. Then instead of watching C-SPAN, they all sit on the floor of the moot caucus room, hugging their stuffed elephants to spend an instructive, inspiring hour with their idol.

"Uncle Newt, Uncle Newt!" said Sara. "Tell us another story about how people lived Before the Contract!"

"Oh, B.C.!" Newt said, settling back in his comfortable leather chair. "That reminds me of a story George Bush once told me over a bag of pork rinds...."

THE THREE LITTLE PIGS
AND THE PERILS OF
SUBSIDIZED HOUSING

ack in the days of the Welfare State, there lived three young males of the porcine persuasion. They were very poor and lived in Bed-Stuy with their widowed mother, Fannie Mae. Their father, a police sergeant affectionately known as "Dirty Harry," had been killed in the line of duty at a violent demonstration by gay performance artists. (Harry's assassins only served a few years in the state pen, where they earned law degrees at taxpayers' expense. Upon release, they joined an environmental law firm.)

One day the little pigs were stretched out on the living room couch, watching *Murphy Brown* reruns. Fannie Mae, who had always been ashamed that her boys were raised on government funds, said, "Your father was an honest working man. I didn't raise you to be lazy boars.

Go out into the world and bring home the bacon yourselves."

So the little pigs left home to seek their fortunes through the sweat of their brows. But the road to financial success was dangerous in those times because the liberal agenda laid many perils before swine. "Dad always said the future was in real estate," said the first little pig who headed over to the Federal Goody Two-Shoes Bureau, where he met with his funding counselor, Mr. Wolf.

"I want to build tract housing out of straw," the little pig said.

"Straw?" Mr. Wolf replied. "That's fabulous! We have farm subsidies for surplus grain, and we can subsidize *you* for reducing the surplus. Now how else can we give you money?"

The little pig rubbed his chinny chin chin. "I don't know. I don't think I deserve any."

"Of course you do, of course you do," exclaimed the bleeding heart carnivore. "How about affirmative action? I can't ask your ethnic affiliation, but if you tell me I will hear."

"Pork—the Other White Meat."

"A minority. That's good. Let's see how minor you can be. The fewer you are, the more you get."

"That doesn't seem fair," said the little pig.

"Fair? Fair? We are always fair, no matter how much it costs, no matter whose rights get trampled during the transition to utter equality, regardless of everything. Of course, the majority is not a minority, so most people get nothing, while crackpots, weirdos, criminals, and misfits—people of individualized lifestyles, as we call them—get it all. That may seem confusing, but if you work for big government long enough it begins to make perfect sense."

Mr. Wolf began showering forms and applications on the little pig right and left—small business loan forms, affirmative action forms, Perks for Porks, NEA grants for building a sculptural straw structure, health benefits, maternity leave applications (just in case). . . . In the end, the first little pig was crushed to death under the weight of big government and its misguided benevolence.

"Oops!" said Mr. Wolf. Then the guilty lupine liberal called the EPA and USDA to help clean up the mess, declared his office a Superfund site, and invited some Democratic senators over for a barbecue. Because he had handled the situation with such finesse, Mr. Wolf was promoted to Assistant Deputy to the Assistant Commissioner of the Bureau of Housing Inspection.

The second little pig, who believed in education, decided to build a multicultural liberal arts boarding school for intellectually disadvantaged immigrants—stupid foreigners, we would call them today. He collected a bunch of sticks and plunged right in. Soon he had a wonderful new building, the product of his own honest toil. Then along came Mr. Wolf.

"Have you done an environmental impact study on the consequences of removing all those sticks from the forest floor?"

The second little pig rubbed his chinny chin chin and said no, in fact, he hadn't. "They were just lying there. I didn't think it could do any harm to pick them up."

"Didn't think. *Didn't think*," Mr. Wolf huffed and puffed. "That's why you have a government, to think about wild improbabilities. We think of the utterly impossible and enact it into law."

"So what should I do?"

"I'll tell you what to do. I am part of a regulatory agency. I protect other people from you. I protect you from other people. I protect you from yourself. I make the world safe for democracy by preventing you from doing almost anything that could conceivably be dangerous or objectionable to anyone."

"Well, that sounds okay, I guess," the little pig said doubtfully.

"After the environmental impact study, you need to do a forest re-flooration study on the feasibility of putting new sticks down to restore the ecological balance to what it was before this continent was settled. We would like to increase the wolf population, for example."

The little pig looked distinctly uncomfortable.

"And then we'll need to look at the building codes. You need smoke detectors in the smokehouse. Wheelchair access for disabled predators trying to gain entry to the chicken coop. All signs must be bilingual—English and Pig Latin."

The little pig, trying to comply with this regulatory hogwash, spent weeks getting his building up to code. At last he thought he was ready to open, and Mr. Wolf came for a final inspection. "Oh, one more thing," Mr. Wolf said. "This property isn't zoned for pigs. So I'm afraid you'll have to go. But we do have an important position for someone with your excellent taste and tender sensibilities. . . ."

"So what happened to the second little pig, Uncle Newt?"

"Well, children, he ended up in something they used to call the school lunch program."

"But weren't there three pigs? What happened to the third?"

"The third little pig was really smart. He built a House of Republicans, and that lasted forever."

"Well, kids—what would you like me to read next?"

"How about a Dr. Koop book?" said Mohammed, one of the younger orphans. "I like 'Orrin Hatches an Egg'."

"Uncle Newt, is it true that Dr. Koop used to be the head doctor of our whole country?" asked Janie.

"Yes, he was once the Surgeon General, just like Doctor Kevorkian is now. You know, kids, Dr. Koop wrote a book just for me. Want to hear it?"

THE NEWT IN THE SUIT

by Dr. Koop

The budget was cockeyed,
Yet taxation soared.
So we sat in the House
All through ninety-four.

We Republicans sat there—
Some Democrats, too—
And we worried about
What the voters would do.

The crime rate was frightful.
There were no more jobs.
We were squandering money
On artists and slobs.

So we sat on our asses.
We were only Congress.
Why should people expect us
To clean up this mess?

We looked!
We saw him! Strong. Resolute.
We looked!
We saw him!
The Newt in the Suit!
And he said to us,
"Let's get things back en route.

"We *have* work to do.
Have a contract to sign.
We'll take this election!
The U.S. is *mine*!

"I have legislation to pass,"
Said the Newt,
"I have some great bills,"
Said the Newt in the Suit.
"A lot of great bills.
I will show them to you.
The voters will love us
If we get them through."

But the Clintons said, "No! No!
Make Newt go away.
He should *not* run our Congress
The GOP way.
We do *not* need reform.
We do *not* need new bills.
Things are just fine
As they are on the Hill."

"Look at me!
Look at me now!" said the Newt,
His Contract with America
Pinned to his suit.
"We'll build up defense.
Give artists the ax.
Balance the budget,
While trimming our tax.
Gals will bear babies.
Guys can bear arms.
Cut welfare, school lunches,
Political terms.
And look!
I can hop up and down on the Hill!
And oh, listen, Bill,
I will do what I will!

Look at me!
Look at me!
Oh, look at *me*!
Congress is really
The *right* place to be!
I'll build family relations.
Create some new jobs.
Exclude those foreigners
(Disgusting yobs).
Reinstate Star Wars,
Ignore the U.N.,
Raise wages, kill villains,
Cut pork barrel, and then . . .
Oh, and then, as the Speaker
I will forge a new age,
Usher in the millennium,
And set the stage
For the GOP Eden,
Oh say, can you see?
Where people are governed
And business is free.

"Oh, I *like* it here.
I like this sensation,"
Said the Newt in the Suit
To a stupefied nation.
"There's no social problem

That I cannot fix.
So now let me show you
Some more of my tricks."

And then Newt ran out
And came back with some clowns
And five hundred elephants
To circle the town.
And the liberals in Congress
Cried, "What will we *do*?
And who's going to clean up
That elephant poo?"

But Newt had an answer.
He gave a big wink.
"Welfare mothers, of course!
Who did you think?"

"Tell us another fairy tale about a newt," said Morgan.

"Don't use that word," screamed President Gingrich.

"Newt?"

"No—'fairy'. It's disgusting."

"Oh. Can we hear the story about the Newt Prince? You know, the one where the princess loses her golf ball down a well, and the newt promises to get it back if she'll let him into the House. And then he knocks on the door of the House and she won't let him in, but the electorate says she has to, and then as soon as he gets in, he turns into a prince and lords it over everybody."

"I'm afraid I never heard of it," said Uncle Newt, "but I do have another instructive story that will help you become good little boy and girl citizens."

SNOW WHITE AND THE
SEVEN SENATORS

nce upon a time, during a blizzard that belied environmentalists' sniveling about global warming, the wife of a prominent politician sat in her parlor sipping vodka and watching *Oprah*. As the room swirled around in a riot of colors, she had a vision that one day she would bear a child who was made of all minorities together; the great American melting pot in one single omni-ethnic being. Then she passed out.

Not long afterward, the lush had a daughter. Whether it was because she had slept with everyone in sight as a hippy college student, or because she drank during pregnancy, or because prenatal testing had caused some genetic mutation, or for some other incomprehensible anti-creationist neo-Darwinian scientific claptrap reason, her child was indeed the perfect multicultural infant. She was all races, creeds, and beliefs rolled into one and called Snow White, an artsy-fartsy name derived from some Bohemian fairy tale.

Then the mother went off to the Betty Ford Clinic and was never seen again.

The politician divorced the pathetic old drunk in absentia and married a nice, new trophy wife, a former centerfold whose junior college degree (in cosmetology) gave her delusions of intellectual grandeur. The one-time Miss April thought she was the most beautiful gal in Washington, and because she still clung to the ambition expressed in her biography—right next to the staples—that she wanted "to help people," she hoped that one day she would be appointed head of the Department of Health and Human Services.

Every day after she dropped her husband at the Capitol Building she walked over to the Reflecting Pool and asked,

"Water, water, on the Mall,

Who's the goodest of them all?"

The Reflecting Pool would always burble back, "You are."

And of course she believed it, because she knew that nothing in Washington ever lied.

Meanwhile Snow White grew bigger and prettier and smarter with each passing year. In spite of daycare, television, popular music, and the educational system, she taught herself reading, writing, and arithmetic. She studied the seven great works of conservative political theory, invested wisely in the stock market, formed a Young Republican Club, and went to church every Sunday.

Finally, the day came when Miss April asked the Reflecting Pool who was the goodest of them all and the

Reflecting Pool replied, "It ain't you, babe."

Miss April was furious. From that moment she hated Snow White and vowed to get rid of her. She summoned the director of the Peace Corps and asked that Snow White be dispatched to some Third World hell hole where she would rot away from exotic diseases, or be eaten, or be clubbed to death by some of the many peoples of the world who resent America's patronizing benevolence.

But the Peace Corps director took pity on Snow White and instead he dropped her off by a wooded suburban development on the outskirts of Georgetown.

Snow White was terrified, but nearby she saw a quaint little cottage. She walked up the path and tapped on the door. No answer. She pushed gently and the door swung open. There stood an elegant table laid with the finest china and silver. A jeroboam of fine champagne stood next to each place. The sideboard sagged under the weight of cold quayle with an apple in his mouth. On the far side of the room were seven little beds, each neatly made up with satin sheets. Now White realized that she had wandered into the Democratic Senate Whoopee Committee's retreat.

Snow White was so hungry and tired that she tasted the food and wine. Then she lay down on the nearest bed, but it was not quite comfortable. She tried them all, one after the other, and finally fell asleep on the seventh.

When it was quite dark, the occupants of the house came home. They were seven little liberal Senators—Needy,

Greedy, Healthy, Wimpy, Whiney, Lefty, and Ted—who spent their days in Washington undermining family values and tearing apart the moral fabric of society. As soon as they turned on the lights they realized that someone had broken in.

"G. Gordon Liddy!" said one.

"My damn constituents!" said another.

"The CIA!" said a third.

"I call her first! She's mine!" said Ted, who had spotted Snow White in his bed.

The next morning the Senators told Snow White that if she washed, cooked, cleaned, mended their clothes, made their beds, and did, oh, perhaps a few other things, they would support her completely at taxpayer's expense, perhaps through a hefty grant from the National Endowment for the Humanities. "*We're* human, aren't we?" said Needy.

"Almost," Snow White agreed.

Every morning the seven Senators went off to dig for gold on Capitol Hill. As they left Snow White, they warned her that she should not open the door for anyone, not for Miss April, who was still out to get her, or for members of the press, who were out to get everyone else.

And, indeed, Miss April had gone back to the Reflecting Pool in triumph after ridding herself of Snow White, and asked:

"Water, water, on the Mall,

Who's the goodest of them all?"

And the Pool told her, "Snow White, of course." So Miss April used her husband's influence, and the FBI and CIA and

ATF combed the world and tapped every phone and opened every envelope and spied on every citizen until they discovered the whereabouts of Snow White.

Then Miss April disguised herself as a humble, hard-working, quaint peddler selling organically grown produce to yuppies from the back of a pick-up truck.

"How about an apple, dearie?" she said when Snow White opened the door. "No Alar."

But Snow White hesitated. She had mixed feelings about street vendors. Though they were admirably enterprising, they had an unfair advantage over storeowners who paid rent, utilities, insurance, and other overhead.

"You know what they say, dearie," the cunning Miss April said, changing her patter to appeal to the conservative young woman. "'An apple a day keeps the doctor away.' Apples are like medicine. Therefore, every apple you buy helps the pharmaceutical industry and will also aid in the fight against health care reform."

This pitch convinced Snow White that the aging hippie vendor really had her heart in the right place. So she took the apple, bit into it, and promptly fell down dead.

When the Senators returned home and found Snow White's corpse, they were very upset. Through a group of leftist scientists who had been leaking national secrets to the Russians for many years under the guise of intellectual sharing in the world scientific community, they contacted the now unemployed Russian embalmers who had preserved

Lenin under glass. They pumped Snow White full of preservatives, pickled her in fungicides, and applied a thin coating of lifelike cosmetics.

Then the Senators checked Snow White into the finest medical center in America, where she was hooked up to the most expensive life-support systems imaginable, and said that she was just in a permanent vegetative state. With diabolical liberal guile, the Senators next petitioned to have her disconnected so that she could die with dignity, which roused all right-thinking Americans to rally to Snow White's defense.

A dead body was thus kept on life support for six years at taxpayers' expense—the ultimate liberal health care dream. In the end the Senators were so inspired by their success that they nominated Snow White as the first female presidential candidate. There were, after all, several precedents for electing virtually lifeless presidents and allowing them to serve out full terms. Moreover, an electoral campaign would be much easier to run if the candidate herself did not interfere with party policy.

Snow White won by a landslide.

HILL AND BILL

Hill and Bill
Went up the Hill
For health care legislation.
Surgeon Gen
Got flaky then,
And touted masturbation.

Group sing time is one of the most popular activities at the orphanages. Uncle Newt and his staff have spent a long time creating new standards for all to enjoy.

"Hee Haw, kids! What time is it?"
"It's Newt-enanny time!"
"What's that? I didn't hear you."
"It's Newt-enanny time!"
"Yep—get ready for the Orphan Sing-Along!"

NEWT-ENANNY TIME—
THE ORPHAN SING-ALONG

HOUSE, HOUSE FOR A CHANGE

TO THE TUNE OF "HOME ON THE RANGE"

Oh give me a House
Where there ain't any louse
And the dear, dear GOP reigns,
Where seldom is heard
The dreaded L-word,
And the sky's deee-regulated all day.
House, House for a change
Where values and morals do reign,
Where seldom is heard
The dreaded L-word,
And the sky's deee-regulated all day.

RUSH LIMBAUGH
TO THE TUNE OF "JOHN HENRY"

When Rush Limbaugh was a little baby
A sittin' on his daddy's knee,
He picked up a mike and a few sponsors, too,
Sayin'—gonna talk 'til I'm blue blue blue,
Gonna talk 'til I'm blue.

The Captain said, hey you, Rush Limbaugh—
I'm gonna bring Larry King around.
I'm gonna set him a talkin' right next to you,
Gonna bring your ratings on down down down,
Bring your ratings on down.

So Rush Limbaugh said—tell ya Captain,
You can bring Larry King around
Bring Howard Stern and any other guy
And I'll outtalk them 'til I die die die,
Scream 'em down 'til I die.

I'VE BEEN TEARING DOWN THE AMTRAK
TO THE TUNE OF "I'VE BEEN WORKING ON THE RAILROAD"

I've been tearing down the Amtrak
All the livelong day.
I've been stopping all the engines,
Just to pass the time away.

Can't you hear the federal coffers
Growin' bigger by the day?
Can't you hear the captain shouting,
NO FREE RIDES TODAY!

THIS LAND IS MY LAND
TO THE TUNE OF "THIS LAND IS YOUR LAND"

*T*his land is *my* land,
This land is *my* land,
From the electoral college
To the info highway,
From the golf course fairways
To the Evian water,
This land was made for *me, me, me.*

WHERE HAS GENNY FLOWERS GONE?
TO THE TUNE OF "WHERE HAVE ALL THE FLOWERS GONE?"

*W*here has Genny Flowers gone?
Long time passing.
Where has Genny Flowers gone?
Some time ago.
Where has Genny Flowers gone?
To the tabloids—fun, fun, fun.
When will Bill ever learn?
When will he ever learn?

Where have all the young girls gone?
Long time passing.
Where have all the young girls gone?
Some time ago.
Where have all the young girls gone?
Troopers picked them, every one.
When will Bill ever learn?
When will he ever learn?

A MCDONALD'S RIGHT NEXT TO YOU
TO THE TUNE OF "DAISY, DAISY," OR "A BICYCLE BUILT FOR TWO"

*L*azy, lazy, you in the welfare state
You're half crazy—what's gonna be your fate?
Babies outside of marriage
Don't deserve a carriage
But you'll enjoy
Being employed
At a McDonald's right next to you.

ANITA HILL
TO THE TUNE OF "JOE HILL"

I dreamed I saw Anita Hill
As sane as you and me.
Said I, "Well, Clarence is my friend—
He never did, did he?
He never did, did he?"

Anita said, "Oh, shucks, you're right,
I made it up, you see.
I always wanted CNN
To make a star of me.
To make a star of me."

THE HOKEY POKEY CONTRACT
TO THE TUNE OF "THE HOKEY POKEY"

*Y*ou put the right wing in,
You kick the left wing out,
You put the right wing in,
And you jump and scream and shout.
You do the hokey pokey
And you turn this land around,
And that's what Newt's all about.

The balanced budget's in,
High income taxes out,
Legal reform is in,
And you jump and scream and shout.
You do the hokey pokey
And you turn this land around,
And that's what Newt's all about.

The military's in,
The immigrants are out,
Term limit rules are in,
Which makes old-timers scream and shout.
You do the hokey pokey
And you turn this land around,
And that's what Newt's all about.

Social security's in,
But social welfare's out,
Business incentives are in,
We'll restore our country's clout.
You do the hokey pokey
And you turn this land around,
And that's what Newt's all about.

Oh, execution's in,
To take the bad guys out,
And family values are in,
And we'll spread 'em all about.
You do the hokey pokey
And you turn this land around,
And that's what Newt's all about.

Miss Lucy Had a Baby
To the tune of "Miss Lucy Had a Baby"

Miss Lucy had a baby.
She named him Johnny Doe.
She sent him off to public school
To see what he could know.

He didn't learn to read or write.
No one seemed to care.
The junkies and agnostic kids
Threw him down the stairs.

Miss Lucy called the Clintons.
Miss Lucy called the nurse.
Miss Lucy called the party
With the endless welfare purse.

In walked the Clintons,
In walked the nurse,
In walked the party
With the endless welfare purse.

"Disadvantaged," said the Clintons,
"Hyperactive," said the nurse,
"Underfunding," said the party
With the endless welfare purse.

"Appoint committees," said the Clintons,
"Do a CAT scan," said the nurse,
"Raise taxes," said the party
With the endless welfare purse.

Another screw-up for the Clintons,
A bonus for the nurse,
A trillion dollars for the party
With the endless welfare purse.

The voters threw out Clinton,
Medicare cuts got the nurse,
And Newt Gingrich nailed the party
With the endless welfare purse.

The orphans stopped singing, and Uncle Newt was still humming as his aides collected the songsheets.

"Gosh—all that music reminds me of a story I know about a famous troubadour," he said.

PRO BONO, THE PIED PIPER
OF PALM SPRINGS

ong ago, when television variety series were still popular, there lived a clown named Pro Bono. He wore his black hair very long, and he was often dressed in floppy ruffled shirts and brightly colored bell-bottom trousers. He was married to a chanteuse, and even though she was a bleeding heart liberal, together they somehow managed to enchant a whole kingdom with a weekly hour of idle chatter, silly skits, and rock songs. But then their ratings slipped, and his chanteuse wife left him to run around with tattooed bikers and make infomercials for hair tonics.

Distraught and disoriented, Pro Bono wandered in the desert for a very long time. His hair grew even longer, and his bell bottoms became frayed. He was on the verge of death when he came upon a fabulous oasis. It was the village of Palm Springs, a good Republican bastion where the rich could feel at ease using millions of gallons of water to maintain their lush golfing greens.

Dehydration had addled the once-famous Bono, who took his wireless microphone out of his pocket and began warbling his greatest hit, "Et Tu, Babe," at the top of his lungs. A young girl, Chastity Sue, became enchanted by his music and took him to her house, where she dressed him in a brand new lime green Nehru suit. Her father was a wealthy manufacturer, and he saw potential in the singing clown.

"I know this looks like a safe place to live," said the manufacturer, "but we're being beset upon by hordes of federal bureaucrats looking for ways to regulate our lives. I don't know where they're coming from, but my guess is the Eastern Sierras, where all those hippie environmentalists live. Since most of them are refugees from the sixties, I think they would like your music. Could you help us out by luring them to the edge of town, where we have several psychedelically painted buses waiting to whisk them to Washington?"

"What will you give me in return?" asked Pro Bono.

"Well, I know you'd like a movie career, or at least another prime time television slot," said the manufacturer. "We have a lot of producers with vacation houses in town, and I will speak to them about getting you your own show or a leading role in a major motion picture."

"Groovy!" said the clown, who immediately began wandering down Main Street, poking into federal offices and performing earnest songs. He sauntered along singing "Blowin' in the Wind" and "Puff the Magic Dragon" and "Hey Mr. Tambourine Man." He walked and warbled "We

Shall Overcome" and "Alice's Restaurant" and "Draft Dodger's Rag."

Like zombies, the liberal bureaucrats emerged from their offices, flung off their ties and pantyhose, and followed Pro Bono in a long swaying line. Some of them rolled marijuana joints that the town had provided free of charge at stands along the way. In less than two hours, they were aboard the hot pink, green, and purple buses and on their way to Washington, where they all became volunteers for ineffectual activist groups.

Pro Bono was excited that his performance had gone over well and went to collect his reward from the manufacturer.

"How about my new TV show or my film role?" he asked.

The manufacturer seemed a little nervous. "Well," he said, "I asked around, and it turns out that you're just not hot enough to pull an audience. I'm afraid you're a has-been, and no one is ready to stake your comeback."

"So what am I going to get, then, for ridding you of your liberal vermin?"

"How about a gift certificate from the local pasta store?"

"No way!" cried Bono the Clown. "I can sing other songs, too, you know."

Then he started out to the outskirts of town, where he posed outside large manses singing Cole Porter and Noel Coward tunes. The rich people began to follow him in droves, all the way to the airport, where they began boarding planes for Aspen and Litchfield and Southampton.

The town fathers became panicky as they watched their tax base evaporate. They rushed out to the airport to see if it was too late to save their standard of lifestyle.

"Is there anything else we could give you, anything else you want?" they asked Pro Bono.

"Make me mayor," said the clown, and they did. He was a very good mayor. After that he went to Washington as a congressman, where he was a good Republican clown who looked after the interests of the people from Palm Springs.

ABC's for GOP's

A's for America, land of the free,
B's for the Budget we'll balance: you'll see,
C's for the Contract that we signed with you,
D is for Bob Dole, the good and the true,
E is for Elephant, our party mascot,
F's for the Family Values we've got,
G is for Government, cut by one-third,
H is for Hatch, Hyde, and Helms and their herd,
I's for Information, which will make us great,
J is for the new Jobs we'll create,
K is for Kassebaum, Alf Landon's kid,
L is for Liberals and the dumb things they did,
M is for Money earned the old-fashioned way
N's for our friends at the dear NRA
O is for Orphans in their Boys Town cities
P's for Political Action Committees
Q is for Queers—we don't like them much,
R is for Reagan (we call him "Dutch")
S is for States looking out for their own,
T's cutting Taxes right down to the bone,
U is for Unfunded Mandates we hate
V is the line-item Veto debate
W is for Welfare—what can we say—
X is for X-ing it out right away,
Y is the voters' "Yes!" to our Contract,
Z is the liberal Zoo that you sacked.

"Now I'm going to tell you a story about what happens when little boys and girls walk alone in the woods," said Uncle Newt as the orphans drew closer.

"What are woods?" asked Kelly.

"Woods are unripe lumber," said the President.

HANSEL AND GRETEL
AND CRUMMY DAYCARE

here once were two children named Hansel and Gretel who had what old-time liberals called "working parents." Their daddy was a very hardworking executive for a lumber concern, and it was understandable that he had to devote himself to life at the office. But their mother could have stayed home with them—she just had some cockamamie idea about fulfilling herself. She worked for a pro-choice action group, which is not surprising, since her choice was to spend all day away from her kids.

Before the Contract, America was riddled with places where people used to dump their children—they were called "day-care centers." There were several in Hansel and Gretel's woodland community, and their parents agonized over which had the most advanced finger painting courses.

Finally they chose Gingerbread Cottage, a place that celebrated multicultural diversity and was closed all the time for one obscure holiday after another. Hansel and Gretel didn't get a chance to attend for a few weeks. Yet, since Hansel and Gretel's femi-nazi mother couldn't stay home from work even for a little while, she just left them at home with a stack of Barney Frank the Liberal Dinosaur tapes and told them to fend for themselves.

Then came the first day that Hansel and Gretel would actually attend Gingerbread Cottage daycare. Hansel and Gretel's mother was running late for work.

"I don't have time to drive you over to daycare today, kids, and I might not get there on time to pick you up," she told Hansel and Gretel. "So here are some Pumpernickel Dill bread crumbs—just throw them down as you walk, and then you can find your way back here tonight and watch *Power Rangers* and *Full House* re-runs until I get home."

Hansel and Gretel, who were used to being latch-key children, set off with a huge bag of bread crumbs. They got to daycare reasonably on time, but they realized that their mother had forgotten to pack them lunches.

"Don't worry," said the head teacher Miss Witch. "Our cottage is made of cheese and other dairy products we got for free from the federal government. Whenever you get hungry, you can just break off a piece. We encourage regular eating."

Miss Witch showed Hansel and Gretel the special big pizza ovens where she cooked snacks.

"They're big enough to cook a kid in!" exclaimed Gretel, and Miss Witch laughed.

Next she showed them the special *Sesame Street* finger puppets she used to measure the children's growth.

"What's 'Sesame Street,' Uncle Newt?"
"That was a program that used to be on a channel called PBS—lots of birds and monsters celebrating the minority inner-city culture."
"Sounds boring."
"It was, kids, it was."

Anyhow, Miss Witch slipped a Big Bird finger puppet on Hansel's finger. "When your finger is too fat to fit into this puppet, it's time for you to leave us," said Miss Witch. She told Hansel and Gretel that the teachers had special feasts every few weeks to celebrate a child's nutritional development and good taste.

Hansel and Gretel really liked the Gingerbread Cottage. They spent the day doing crafts projects from El Salvador and learning the lyrics to sixties protest songs. They studied the indigenous folk customs of all sorts of disadvantaged cultures. Miss Witch told them all about the heritage of her people, the witches, who had been oppressed for a long time even though they were naturalists, midwives, and strong women loving other women. Then she introduced Hansel and Gretel to her longtime companion, Candace.

At the end of the day Hansel and Gretel didn't want to go home, which was just as well since some birds had eaten all the bread crumbs anyway and they would never find their way back to their parents' condominium. Their mother wasn't surprised when they weren't home. She had been hoping all along that they would go off and find their own apartment. After awhile she forgot that she had even had children—now she had more time to work and could go on Caribbean vacations with her husband.

After a month, Miss Witch and Candace cooked Hansel Cajun-style. Then a week later they experimented with a Thai recipe for Gretel.

At this point, one of the orphans began to cry.

"You're scaring me, Uncle Newt! Why did they have to be eaten?"

Newt laughed heartily. "Now, now. That could never happen to you. Your mommies don't work. Why, you don't even have mommies! But just remember the moral of this story: Working mothers don't work. People are hungry for the way things used to be. Greed and power devour traditional family values...."

Then President Gingrich left the orphans for a quick lunch break, and we saw him chuckling over his pizza.

WEE WILLIE CLINTON

Wee Willie Clinton runs through the town,
Upstairs and downstairs in his nightgown,
Tapping all the troopers, looking for a fox,
"Is the babe in my bed,
For now it's ten o'clock?"

"Uncle Newt, is it true that now, thanks to your Cyber-Presidency, we can talk to orphans all over the world?"

"Yes, kids—through my new project, Orphans-on-Line, you can surf the Internet, trading your hopes, secrets, and dreams with other unfortunates such as yourselves.

"Here, just take a look," said the President, booting little Jimmy out of his lap so he could boot up his laptop. "Now you can get access to Charlotte's Worldwide Web with just a few keystrokes."

Then the President typed:

```
http.llww.orph.gov.waif***369/the
goose drank wine/the monkey chewed
tobacco(lobby) on the street car
line//eeny meeney miny mo/ catch an
orphan by the toe [ ENTER ]
```

and a beautiful graphic of Oliver Twist popped onto the screen.

"Ah ... here we are ... the Orphan Home Page."

"Cooool, Uncle Newt," said Max, "We're going to love being Cyber-Orphans. But while you're here won't you tell us another story?"

THE PRINCESS
AND THE PEANUT

nce upon a time there was a big law firm
that specialized in product liability
litigation. The firm sued everyone in sight.
No matter how good a product was, no
matter how beautifully it was made, how
safely it was crafted, how carefully
designed, the firm would always find something that could
somehow be dangerous or scary or annoying to someone. Then
the firm would sue the manufacturer and win lots of money.

The lawyers were very happy. They felt that they were
making the world safe. They were also getting very rich by
defending the poor and downtrodden, but they knew they
deserved it. They sat in their castles sipping cognac and smoking
cigars, thinking about how much good they were doing.

One day the senior partner of the firm decided that they
needed a new partner. But he insisted that she had to be a real
princess, just to maintain the multicultural, gender-balanced,
socioeconomically homogenized mix required if they ever

wanted to do any juicy federal litigation.

Lawyers applied for the job by the dozens—mean lawyers, greedy lawyers, brilliant lawyers whose minds had been hopelessly warped by the modern legal climate. Some of them had sued their own parents for raising them to be ruthless lawyers and social outcasts. One had sued herself and won, and now was suing herself again for incompetence because she had also lost. Several sued the law firm for discrimination after they were turned down for the partnership. But the senior partner could not be sure that any of them was a real princess.

One stormy night another candidate arrived. Her makeup streamed down her face in the rain (defective merchandise), seeped into her eyes (pain and suffering), dripped onto her clothes (personal property damage). She said she was the princess to end all princesses. She could sue anyone, she said.

We'll just see about that, thought the senior partner and his office manager, an old queen. What's the greatest challenge? Who's the most perfect, unassailable person imaginable?

Jimmy Carter may have been an ineffectual president, but since leaving office he had grown so spectacularly *good*—with his houses for the poor, his poetry, his great big warm smile, and mediating abilities that could charm the most belligerently inclined Third World terrorists into sitting down for a friendly chat—that no one but a supreme princess of litigation could possibly manage to sue him.

"Nail Jimmy Carter!" said the senior partner.

So the princess went to see Jimmy Carter. She explained

that she was very poor, and came from a far-off land so disadvantaged that cartographers would not put it on maps. She spoke on behalf of the noble indigenous population, who were tormented and oppressed by a despotic ruler backed by a strategic alliance between the former KGB and the CIA. They desperately needed Jimmy Carter to mediate.

Jimmy Carter took the princess into his own house, where he fed her and let her sleep on the softest bed he could find. He piled twenty mattresses and twenty feather beds on top of each other to make sure that this persecuted soul would have a little rest at last.

But under the bottom mattress lay a single peanut, that a sharecropper's child had hidden there for his dinner.

In the morning the princess woke in a towering rage. When Jimmy Carter humbly came to serve her breakfast with his own hands, she demanded, "How do you expect me to sleep in a dump like this? I was scared to death I was going to topple off this pile of bedding and kill myself. And this mattress! I don't know what's in it, but I'm sure I have several broken bones and have suffered permanent internal injuries. I'll see you in court."

Even with a jury, the firm succeeded in reducing the goodly former president to abject poverty and disgrace. The princess was made a full partner. And the peanut can now be seen in a glass case in the lobby of the local Bar association.

"Uncle Newt, what was multicultural diversity?" asked Frank.

"Well, we used to actually allow foreigners to come live in this country, but then it got out of hand. They started wanting us to celebrate their fool holidays and see things from their point of view. Thank God we put an end to that. But we're still interested in selling our American goods to people in other lands."

"So we don't want them to live here," said Frank, "but it's great if they shop here, right?"

"Exactly," said Uncle Newt, beaming. "Let me tell you a little story about how hard we worked to stimulate the economy with exports. . . ."

THE INTEL ENGINE
THAT COULD

hug, chug, chug. Puff, puff, puff. Ding-dong, ding-dong. The American economy rumbled along the tracks, happily carrying its jolly load of goods.

There were knick-knacks, sitcoms, airplanes, weapons, coal, medicines, agricultural machines, textiles, tobacco, microchips, and chemicals.

There were also lots of delicious things to eat—wheat, corn, rice, and Big Macs. Everything the world could want.

The American engine was carrying all these things to people around the world, and many of the best things over Mount Fuji to the good little boys and girls of Japan.

Then all of a sudden the economy stopped with a jerk. It would not go. The deficit was too high. Trade barriers stood in the way. America tried and tried, but the wheels of industry would not turn.

What would all the good little boys and girls of Japan do without the fruits of American labor and the products of Yankee ingenuity?

"Here comes a big old Hollywood engine," said an entrepreneur, jumping out on the tracks. "Maybe he will help us."

So all the businessmen and exporters and bankers and stockbrokers shouted together: "Please, old Hollywood engine, won't you please help us over Mount Fuji, which stands as a symbol of unfair Japanese trade restrictions against a free world economy?"

The big old engine used to be strong and brave and would stand up for people's rights, at least in the movies, but now he was feeble, he had to touch up his fading black paint every day, and his memory wasn't what it once was. "I can't remember how to help you," the big old engine said. "So I just have to say no."

How dismal the economy and all the businessmen were!

Then the entrepreneur called out, "Look! Here comes another engine! A big, tall Texas engine! Let's ask him to help us."

The big, tall engine came up, all splendidly decorated with a thousand points of light, blowing smoke, and pulling a very silly little tender behind.

"Please, big tall engine," called out all the businessmen and exporters and bankers and stockbrokers, "won't you help our economy and get us over Mount Fuji so that all the good little Japanese girls and boys will have American products to buy?"

The big, tall engine said, "Well . . . " And he dithered and talked, and hemmed and hawed. He poked at the economy here, and tugged at it there, and carried on so much while doing so little that finally everyone grew tired of waiting. The big engine's tender cried out in a tiny, high-pitched voice, "What about me? I can help, too!" But no one paid any attention. "You're no locomotive!" said one investor.

All the businessmen were very sad. They thought the economy would never go.

"Look! Here comes another engine!" said the entrepreneur.

A stubby little donkey engine from Arkansas puffed up, shoving french fries into his firebox. He said, "I'm not sure I can make it up Fuji by myself. But I'll appoint some other engines—engines of all shapes and sizes, engines of all ages and colors, steam engines, diesel engines, electric engines, solar engines. . . . It will take time, though, and some of them won't work, so we'll have to appoint other engines to replace them. Oh, it will take time. It will take time."

But the good little boys and girls of Japan could not wait for the games and bluejeans and Cadillacs and fast food from America.

So the entrepreneur went to Intel, which could bring information technology to everyone. And he went to aerospace companies who could take people to the stars. And he went to several other Fortune 500 companies with proprietary cutting edge technologies, and they formed a gigantic Political Action Committee to force the government to be answerable to the needs of corporate America.

"Oh, Intel engine," called all the businessmen and exporters and bankers and stockbrokers, "Will you pull us over Fuji and into the heart of Japan? Otherwise the good little boys and girls of Japan will only have Sony and Hitachi and Toshiba and Mitsubishi to play with. They will have to eat seaweed instead of fried chicken. They will have to watch Kurosawa movies instead of *The Lion King*."

The Intel engine saw the tears and aching wallets of the businessmen and took pity on them. The Intel engine hitched itself to the economy and said, "Republi-CAN. Republi-CAN. Republi-CAN. Republi-CAN."

Slowly, slowly, the economy moved up Mount Fuji. "Republi-CAN. Republi-CAN. Republi-CAN. Republi-CAN."

Faster and faster. Up and up went the Intel engine and the economy, over the top of the mountain and the trade barriers.

"Hurray, hurray," cried all the business folk. "The people of Japan will be very happy that you helped us bring our goods into their country."

And the Intel engine and all the rest of corporate America smiled as they raced down the mountain. They seemed to say, "And so they should. And so they should. And so they should. And so they should."

HICKERY TRICKERY DICK

Hickery Trickery Dick,
That pardon sure did stick.
By the time he died
We forgot he lied,
Hickery Trickery Dick.

"Uncle Newt, is it true that in the past, school children weren't allowed to worship God?"

"Yes, kids. You see, the liberals thought that the best way to ensure religious freedom was to keep people from talking about God. Only a few years ago, I wouldn't have been able to tell you any Bible stories in a federal facility."

"Not even 'Jonah and the Whale'?" said Kelly, who loved sea stories.

"Especially not 'Jonah and the Whale.' The liberals would have fined God for leaving around a small object like Jonah that an endangered species could choke on."

"So what did the liberals tell stories about?" asked little Sara.

"Oh, they liked whiney things about how women and minorities were oppressed. That reminds me of a story about so-called 'women's issues.'"

CINDERELLA
AND THE GLASS CEILING

nce upon a time there was an orphan named Cinderella. Her mother had died when she was very young, and her father had married an illegal immigrant gal who needed a green card. His new wife had two young daughters of her own who had been supported by government money ever since birth. Unfortunately, Cinderella's father died soon after the marriage from a stomach ailment brought on by consuming his wife's spicy cooking.

After getting a huge settlement from the company that had manufactured the cayenne pepper she used, Cinderella's stepmother bought a big prewar co-op apartment for the family. Each of the stepsisters had her own room, but Cinderella was forced to sleep in the walk-in linen closet. The sisters took Suzuki violin lessons and went to dance classes while Cinderella stayed home and cleaned the enormous apartment, polishing its hardwood floors and oiling the granite counters of the newly redecorated eat-in kitchen.

Because they were from a minority group, the stepsisters got full scholarships to Harvard Business School, even though they really weren't as smart as Cinderella (she had to read their high school diplomas to them), and when they graduated they were both accepted into a special affirmative action program that gave them entry-level executive jobs at Prince Industries, a multi-million-dollar conglomerate.

Cinderella stayed home and continued to clean, but since her stepsisters had moved into their own apartment, she didn't have to pick up their Wonderbras and clean up their makeup from the bathroom sink anymore. Her stepmother didn't give her any money, so she had to figure out what to do for a living. Making the most of what she had, she started her own cleaning business, which she ran from the linen closet with the aid of an old IBM PC Junior her stepsisters left behind. (Her stepmother had used the stepsisters' rooms to build herself a large personal gym and weight-lifting center.)

One day the stepsisters came over, all excited.

"Mom, you're not going to believe it! Mr. Prince the CEO is having a huge cocktail party for all the junior executives at Prince Industries," said one. "Can you help us pick out the right power suits to wear?"

"Can family members come too?" asked Cinderella, who had always wanted to see where her stepsisters worked.

The stepsisters started laughing.

"Are you kidding?" said the oldest one. "You smell like Windex. You don't have any silk blouses to wear."

"But here's some good news," said the younger stepsister. "They were looking around for someone to do special cleaning for the party, and I gave them your number. Don't say I never did anything for you. By the way, can you read the time on the invitation for me? I never learned my numbers."

Cinderella was upset. Her sisters were so stupid and shallow, yet they kept getting these great opportunities. She tried not to think about it and made more calls to her cleaning service clients.

On the day of the cocktail party, she showed up early and was assigned the task of clipping off stray threads from the oriental carpets in the executive ballroom. While she was bent over her task, a well-dressed middle-aged woman who looked a lot like Governor Christy Whitman appeared.

"Who are you?" asked Cinderella.

"I am your Fairy Mentor," said the woman. "I know you really want to go to this party, and I can help you. Affirmative action can only go so far—what the party needs is a good, smart old-fashioned girl who knows the meaning of work. Besides, that CEO is a catch!"

Then the Fairy Mentor waved her copy of *Swim with the Sharks and Don't Turn into a Pumpkin* over Cinderella's head and she was transformed into a sexually attractive but competent-looking businesswoman, complete with uncomfortable pumps and little gold earrings peeking out from under a conservative but fetching hairstyle.

Cinderella was very excited. She especially liked her new foundation garments. She unbuttoned her blouse to gaze at her bustier from Victoria's Secret. She liked the way it thrust up her breasts, and she couldn't help but fondle the lustrous fabric—

"Uncle Newt, what's a bustier? Why is she taking off her clothes?"
"Umm. Never mind, kids. I was thinking of another book I wrote awhile ago. Back to the story."

So the Fairy Mentor gave Cinderella some tips on networking, and one important piece of advice: "You must leave before the CEO gets up to speak, or I can't guarantee what will happen."

The cocktail party was in full swing when Cinderella entered. All eyes fell on her, even though her suit wasn't an Armani. She was so businesslike that even her stepsisters didn't recognize her. As soon as the CEO spotted her, he made a beeline over to find out which division of Prince Industries she worked for.

"Hello, I'm Mr. Prince, the CEO. You can call me "The," he said, shaking her hand heartily. "I don't believe we've met before. Are you here at headquarters?"

"Oh. I'm not sure exactly what I do," said Cinderella, batting her eyelashes. "I really don't care much about my career. What I've always wanted was a man I could take care of, and a family. I could imagine having my husband come home and I would fix him a nice dinner and then rub his back while he talked about his troubles at the office."

"Really?" said Mr. Prince. "Could I show you my new paper shredder? It's in my office."

So Cinderella and the CEO went into his private office, and he found himself irresistibly drawn to this fetching young unambitious woman. They were just about to kiss when he pushed her away.

"I love that smell in your hair. Windex, isn't it? You know, I've never really admitted it to anyone before, but I have a Glass Ceiling here at the office, and it is slightly smudged, so I'm afraid the other women will see that I had it installed, especially those affirmative action babes. Would you mind helping me clean it?"

With that, he got a small stepladder and helped Cinderella onto it. He lifted her up gently and rubbed her head back and forth on the Glass Ceiling. But he must have pushed too hard, because her head made a small indentation in the ceiling.

Just as they were coming back down the ladder, the CEO's personal assistant knocked on the door to let him know that it was time for his speech.

As soon as Mr. Prince reached the podium, Cinderella panicked. He started to speak and she ran out of the room. While she was waiting for the elevator, she noticed that her power suit had vanished and she was dressed in the navy blue sweatsuit she always wore for heavy cleaning jobs.

She arrived home dejected. Her sisters stopped by a few hours later to tell their mothers all about the party and how they thought they would surely be getting promotions any day now, especially since Mr. Prince had announced a new remedial communications seminar that would help them learn how to dial the telephone.

Meanwhile, Mr. Prince the CEO could hardly sleep that night. No one had ever run out on a speech of his. When he came into the office the next day, he looked up and saw that his ceiling had been damaged. Angry, he wrote a memo ordering every woman in the company to come to his office. He wanted to find and fire the woman who had made a dent in his Glass Ceiling.

One by one, the well-coifed female executives ascended a ladder, but not one of their heads fit the indentation. After awhile Mr. Prince gave up trying to find the mysterious woman, but he cancelled the company's affirmative action program just to make sure something like that would never happen again.

One day he was working late at the office when a young cleaning woman knocked timidly on his door. It was Cinderella, who had gotten a contract to clean Prince Industries offices. The CEO hardly looked up as she came in to empty his wastebasket. But a familiar smell roused him.

"Windex!" he said. "Could it be? Is it really you?"

He grabbed Cinderella and hoisted her up by her ankles. From below he could see that her head fit the ceiling indentation perfectly.

"Yes, I'm the one who messed up your ceiling," cried Cinderella. "But I promise I'll pay for it—if you'll let me keep my job cleaning your office."

"But you're the only woman who ever almost went through the Glass Ceiling here," said Mr. Prince, his eyes misting up. "Why, I should promote you to executive vice president. I should give you a corner office."

Cinderella continued crying. "I don't want that. I just want to be a wife and mother."

"And you can be. If you promise not to sue me for sexual harassment for touching your ankles, I'll make you my wife. You are the most beautiful and compliant woman I've ever met. I promise after we're married, you'll never have to work again. Of course, you wouldn't be able to work here, anyway, since we have anti-nepotism rules."

So Cinderella married The Prince. He had a new safety glass ceiling installed in his office and they lived happily ever after.

Summer is that special time when enterprising orphans can supplement their usual diets of gruel and Kool-Aid with fresh vegetables and fruit. Every year the orphanages hold Republican Victory Garden contests to see who can grow the most produce for the White House kitchen.

Last year's winners, residents of the Barry Goldwater State Orphanage in Flagstaff, Arizona, took President Gingrich on a tour of their garden.

"We use lots of pesticides!" said Tracy, proudly displaying her prize tomatoes.

"What have we got here?" asked Uncle Newt, looking at a tall tangle of vines.

"That's my beanstalk," said Terry, a shy nine-year-old who had made his own watering cans out of old milk cartons.

"This is what I like—little people out in their gardens. The heck with food stamps—you kids are on the bean. And that reminds me of a story about another little guy who climbed a stalk and beat a system."

JACK AND THE
BEAN COUNTERS

here was a poor bean farmer named Jack who lived in Iowa and never really understood why he paid so many taxes or why his kids weren't allowed to pray in school. And another thing Jack really couldn't understand was why he never got a chance to do any farming.

Every year he got a letter from a government office saying they would pay him a lot of money not to plant any beans. Once he wrote and asked how he could make money without planting anything, but no one answered back.

"I'm just going to call and find out why they don't want me to plant," he told his wife one year as she grabbed the check from him.

"What a waste of time," she said.

And she was right. Poor Jack tried and tried to reach the government to tell them he wanted to work and plant his fields, but none of the officials could understand why he didn't just shut up and take the money.

"The Russians and Mexicans can send us plenty of beans. We are not legume-challenged," said one of the more patient bureaucrats. "Now, why don't you just go down to the mall and stop worrying?"

But Jack wanted to have something to do, so one night he took out a packet of beans and, using the ornamental hoe paperweight his wife had given him from the Sharper Image catalog, he tilled a tiny patch of soil outside his window and dumped the seeds into the ground.

The next day Jack's wife woke him up screaming.

"Now see what you've done!" said she. "You've gone and done some planting, haven't you, and now the government won't take care of us anymore!"

The beans had sprouted into a magnificent beanstalk reaching all the way up to the ozone layer. (In fact, some kindly local official had already installed blinking red lights toward the top to prevent aircraft collisions.)

"But dear, can't you see—you're looking out the Window of Opportunity," said Jack, gazing out at his super crop. "I'm going to climb that stalk and see what's up in the sky."

He climbed and he climbed.

No wonder it took so long for mail to reach him from there! No wonder his phone calls went unanswered! Big Big Government was a long, long way up—a kind of pie in the sky place far removed from the little people. Everything up there was giant and hard to get into, and there was a beltway around the city where the residents traveled around and around in foreign cars all day.

Jack came to a giant white house—a palace, really, and he knew that was where the Head Giant lived. There were guards all around, but Jack was tiny enough to slip in through a mousehole.

Well, the very first thing to greet him was a giant black and white cat. Jack thought he was a goner, but when photographers arrived to do a special shoot starring the cat, he was able to run away.

He scurried into the first room he saw and came upon a giant golden harp. The harp was playing and singing the smuttiest songs Jack had ever heard. It made him blush to hear such dirty ditties.

"Now why does the Head Giant keep a slutty harpy like you around?" he asked the golden instrument.

"I am an artist!" she replied. "I get funding from Big Big Government to sing about all my own bodily pleasures. I strip off my strings and parade around. I am officially known as a performance artist. I've never had to work a day in my life."

Just then the whole floor of the giant white house shook, and Jack heard the mighty voice of the Head Giant returning from another press junket.

"Fee fie foe fum. I smell the bull of a congressman!"

"Watch out," warned the harp. "He's been really upset lately, what with the Republican freshman suggesting that we actually try to relate to the little people. He's even worried about losing me."

Then the giant entered, holding a big hen who was wearing a little T-shirt that said TAXES. The giant was squeezing the hen with one hand while eating french fries with another.

"Lay, lady, lay. Lay, goddamit!" yelled the giant.

"Hey, that line might work with other girls, but not with me," huffed the hen. "You can squeeze all you want, but I don't think I have many golden eggs left in me."

Golden eggs! Jack thought about how much his wife would love him if only he could bring her a golden harp and golden eggs. He vowed right then and there to steal both precious things and take them down to the world of the little people.

Night came and the giant got sleepy. From time to time some official bean counters came in to tell him what was happening in all the big offices of Big Big Government. He ate a few more french fries, drank a few beers, and sang a few Bubba giant songs. Then he watched his wife, Giantess, and his daughter, Giantess Junior, on CNN getting some Third World country named after themselves.

Finally the giant fell asleep. Jack crept up with a huge sack, stuffed the hen and the harp inside, and bounded down the beanstalk. At the bottom of the stalk a crowd of well-wishers had gathered, buzzing in excitement.

"You've returned our taxes!" they yelled, grabbing the hen. "At last we'll have our nest eggs back!"

"Who needs those leftist commie artists anyway?" they exclaimed, putting the harp to work as one of the performers at a Chuckie Cheese pizza restaurant.

Jack was ecstatic. He ran to tell his wife about his adventures in the land of Big Big Government. But when he got home he found a note:

Dear Jack,

Sorry, but while you were gone a federally funded photographer happened by. He said he was taking pictures of all the refrigerators in the area and then he made love to me on the kitchen table and told me I was a part of the universe and belonged to him because he was wild and free. So I'm leaving with him to live off the profits of his upcoming book, The Fridges of Madison County.

Hope you had a nice trip.
Jackie
Your (former) wife

Jack was devastated for a couple of days, but he still believed in family values, so he pulled himself together, found a trophy wife, and ran for Congress.

"Kids, my mother used to tell me a story about this bitch——er, witch——named Hillary. She was a cold woman. Want to hear it?"

"Yes, yes Uncle Newt! We love cold bitch stories!"

HILLARY
THE SNOW QUEEN

nce upon a time there was a mirror, and a queen who loved to gaze into it. Her name was Hillary, and she had a hair problem. For a long time she solved the problem by putting on a magic headband that kept her hair away from her face and let everyone know how intellectual she was. But then her husband became king and some of the court reporters said the headband just wouldn't do anymore.

Hillary tried. She let the royal hairstylists cut her hair and perm her hair and frost her hair. Of course, most of them were homosexuals, and what do they know about making a woman look good?

Every time Hillary got a new hairdo, she would go out in public and the press would send a cold blast of criticism her way. After awhile, Hillary had tried every type of hairdo imaginable, but nothing helped. The people just didn't like her. That's because, underneath, her brain remained the same.

She was what they used to call "assertive." In fact she was downright uppity. And she was too smart to make sense of why everybody cared about her hair so much.

One day when Hillary was at the hairdresser's, she looked into the mirror and became so angry that the mirror broke into a hundred pieces. One of the pieces lodged in her heart. Her bleeding heart grew colder and colder. So she went to the doctor to see if she could get a prescription to help thaw out her heart or make her care less about social programs.

Hillary found out that the heart medicine prescription cost far too much. She got it into her pointy head that the pharmaceutical companies had too much power, and that they cheated the American public. Part of her brain froze, too. She convinced the King that doctors should work for the government, even if it meant that they wouldn't be able to afford a good summer house. She became so obsessed, she didn't even have time to make up new cookie recipes for ladies' magazines.

A lot of people thought she needed Prozac, or at least First Lady Strength Midol. But Hillary was undeterred by people's opinions. She decided she would dedicate her life to making health care more affordable.

Every time the congressmen of the court would see Hillary coming, they'd mutter, "Uh-oh. Here comes the Snow Job Queen." They couldn't figure out how she planned to make health care accessible to everyone without bankrupting the whole kingdom.

"So what happened? Did she ever unfreeze?"

"No, kids—it's a sad story. She even tried microwave oven treatments, but the public just never warmed up to her. Not only did she remain frozen, she froze up the government, too. Nothing happened until we came along, and then it was like spring!"

"Where is she now?"

"We use her to keep the Budweisers cold at the Republican picnics."

"Okay—what will it be next, kids? I see you've gotten a few more books in since last time. I could read you 'The Very Hungry Congressman', or something from that wonderful new 'Curious George Bush' series."

Trevor, a young orphan with a cardboard sword dangling from his belt, spoke up: "How about a story from, like, really long ago? Stuff with swords and fighting. Like—what's the one with the guy in the green suit, and Maid Marion Berry?"

Uncle Newt chuckled. "Wrong Marion, son. But I can tell you a story about heroic men in times gone by."

THE ADVENTURES OF ROBIN LEACH HOOD

n the days of the kings of yore—Billie Jean King, Rodney King, Burger King—liberal notions of egalitarianism ran amuck. According to the natural order of things, the rich should be rich and the poor should be penniless. "If the good lord intended the poor to have money," one profound thinker of the time remarked, "he would have given them inheritances."

Robin Leach Hood was an investment banker who lived in Sherwood Mews, a luxury community for the rich and famous. Robin's creative manipulation of the market netted him and a few preferred clients enormous and well-deserved sums of money that enabled them to appreciate the natural wonders of this world to the fullest possible extent. Then one day Charles F. Nottingham, an auditor with the IRS, questioned Robin's methods of calculating his taxes, and put a crimp in his lifestyle by throwing him in prison.

In prison Robin did not meet the murderers, thieves, and rapists he expected: They had all been acquitted, pardoned, or paroled because they were insane ("He didn't know he was strangling the old lady, he thought he was squeezing a grapefruit"), socially disadvantaged (the other guy had money in his wallet and he didn't), or represented by a slippery lawyer (the poor deserve free counsel, while the middle class has to pay). Rather he found such upstanding citizens as Little John, founder of a liposuction franchise, Televangelist Tuck, a multimedia ministry mogul, and Will Scarlet, purveyor of high-end athletic clothes and exercise equipment.

It was, to tell the truth, a minimum security, white-collar prison. Robin and Little John met on the golf course when Robin, clad in his trademark Lincoln green sweatsuit, asked the great oaf in front of him to "let the better man play through." Robin and "L.J." were soon flailing at each other with putters, and eventually ended up, dazed and bruised but laughing uproariously, in a water trap, and became bosom buddies for ever after. Robin befriended Televangelist Tuck during the Piggyback Race in the Special Penal Olympics. Prison turned out to be a very positive experience for intelligent, enterprising men such as themselves. Working away at the terminals in their cells late at night they used on-line financial services to amass a new fortune, which they put into a jointly owned corporation, Merry Men Enterprises, Inc.

The night before Robin was scheduled for release, his friends and the guards (or incarceration attendants) threw a farewell party for him in the prison bar's Jollye Olde Englande Roome. The high point of the evening was a shooting match with assault weapons on the prison target range, a contest that Robin won handily.

"Hearken, men," Robin said back in the bar. "We were imprisoned in this bleak and dreadful place because we would not surrender our hard-earned money to the evil tax policies of a corrupt liberal government. What say ye, stout fellows, that when we are free we dedicate ourselves to robbing the poor to give back to the rich what they have earned."

"Hear! Hear!" shouted the assembled men, growing merrier by the minute as they knocked back braces of rare cognac and single malt scotch.

"Hail, Robin!" cheered Little John, drinking deeply of an exotic microbrewery mead. "We will give dignity back to the laboring class by taking away perks for the poor. We will build additions to our houses, throw vast catered banquets, buy costly handmade clothing and furniture, order cases of pre-peeled grapes, and in every way we possibly can create more *real honest work* for the currently unemployed peasant class. Once we have destroyed the welfare system, downtrodden Americans will be willing to work for paltry wages, and we will no longer need to rely on the poor in other lands."

"Verily!" said Will Scarlet. "Let every nation oppress its own poor!"

"Hooray for Robin Leach Hood!" they all shouted. "Put the poor to work, put real criminals in jail, and put the rich back in the lap of luxury where they belong!"

So Robin Leach Hood and Merry Men Enterprises went down in history, their valiant exploits now familiar to all who listen to country and western music. Their independent initiative was finally recognized by the new, reformed government, and they were given cabinet positions, where they could continue their work inside, rather than outside, the law.

SCHOOL LUNCH HOT, SCHOOL LUNCH COLD

School lunch hot,
School lunch cold,
We don't really need school lunch,
So we're told.

Some liked it hot,
Some liked it cold,
Those who devoured it
Were on the public dole.

"Now, children," said Uncle Newt. "Let me tell you another story—it's a bit scary—about the sort of crime that was rampant in some parts of our country before we really figured out how to keep people in line."

"Is this the story of the poor shoemaker who blew away the elves who kept breaking into his shop and messing with the leather he had cut out to make some shoes?" asked Peewee, one of the youngest orphans in the place.

"No, Peewee, though that is one of my own favorite tales. Pow! Pow! Those elves are dead meat. Elf McNuggets, you might say."

The orphans laughed at Uncle Newt's joke.

"No, children," Uncle Newt continued, "I am going to tell you the story of 'The Gingerbread Delinquent', who went on a wild criminal rampage before he was finally brought to justice."

THE GINGERBREAD
DELINQUENT

nce upon a time there was a little old woman and a little old man and they lived by themselves in a little old slum. They had no little boys and no little girls and no family values at all. One day, the little old lady made a gingerbread boy. She believed having a child would be nice and might affirm her female identity. She gave no thought to the responsibility that goes along with bringing new life into the world, even life that consists of mere dough.

The little old woman and the little old man mindlessly decorated the gingerbread boy with advantages they could not afford. They bought him everything he wanted—candy, designer clothes, electronic games, tapes and CDs, then they popped him into the local godless public school hoping that it would turn him into a successful citizen.

One day the little old woman and the little old man went to pick up their gingerbread son at school. When they opened the door, he popped out and ran down the street, laughing and shouting, "Run, run, as fast as you can! You can't catch me, I'm the cool GB man!"

And they could not catch him.

The gingerbread boy ran on and on, and as he needed money to support his molasses habit and extravagant tastes, he soon robbed a milk delivery truck.

"Stop, little gingerbread boy," said the milkman. "Come back here, you thief."

But the little gingerbread boy only laughed and said, "Run, run, as fast as you can! You can't catch me, I'm the cool GB man!"

And the milkman could not catch him.

The little gingerbread boy ran on and on, knocking over banks, drugstores, and racetracks, leaving a trail of wanton crime and destruction in his wake, for he had never learned the difference between right and wrong or the sacred value of private property.

"Stop, little gingerbread boy," the security guards and police all called after him. "Or we'll blast you into a pile of crumbs!"

But the little gingerbread boy only laughed and said, "Run, run, as fast as you can! You can't catch me, I'm the cool GB man!"

And all the security guards and police could not catch him.

Eventually the recipe for the gingerbread boy appeared on *America's Most Wanted*. Then *everybody* was after the baked fugitive variously known as the "Chewy Offender," the "Mafioso Mouthful," or the "Cookie Kingpin of Crime."

But the little gingerbread boy called in to the show and gloated, "Run, run, as fast as you can! You can't catch me, I'm the cool GB man!"

And *America's Most Wanted* could not catch him.

One day the little gingerbread boy came to the Potomac River, where he spent a leisurely afternoon robbing tourists of their wallets and jewelry. Suddenly he noticed House Judiciary Committee chairman Henry Hyde sitting on a bench, watching him.

The little gingerbread boy laughed at Hyde and said, "Run, run, as fast as you can! You can't catch me, I'm the cool GB man!"

"Why," said the crafty Hyde, "I wouldn't dream of catching you. I want to help you."

"Help me?" said the gingerbread boy. "How can *you* help *me?*"

"Well," said the vulpine representative, "I want to build more prisons. I think you could be of service."

"Why would I want to help you build more prisons?"

"More cells means fewer crooks on the streets," said the crafty congressman. "And that, of course, means less competition for you. Get into my limo and we'll discuss it."

"Hmm," said the boy as he climbed gingerly onto the backseat.

"And a smart cookie like you surely knows that there's a fortune to be made in kickbacks on government construction projects," Hyde grinned, showing his big, sharp teeth.

"You're right," said the gingerbread boy, moving closer. "Let's go."

The limo whisked them off to a big fund-raising event. A banner over the ballroom door said, "TAKE A BITE OUT OF CRIME."

The foxy Hyde took the gingerbread boy up to the stage, pounded his gavel, and shouted, "All right, the anti-crime auction is now open, all proceeds to go to the new prison building fund. What will you bid for pieces of this delicious gingerbread boy?"

The bidding went on fast and furious all afternoon. "Oh, no!" said the little gingerbread boy as the total passed the $1 million mark. "I am half gone!" An hour later, as the fund reached $3 million, he said, "Oh, no! I am three-quarters gone!" And by the time the bidding was over and the full total for a brand new correctional facility had been raised, the little gingerbread boy was completely silent.

I Have a Federal Shadow

I have a little shadow that goes in and out with me,
And what can be the use of him is more than I can see.
But as federal employees, we're supposed to duplicate,
And never do alone what can be done by six or eight.

A funny thing about him——he's as stupid as they come.
The private sector'd never give a job to anyone so dumb.
On his good days he just sits and gazes blankly at the wall,
But most times he forgets, and doesn't come to work at all.

He hasn't got a notion what we're really here to do.
He's just thinking of his pension,
And his health insurance, too.
The purpose of the government, he told me with a grin,
Is to create a couple million jobs for idiots like him.

"It's almost time to leave, kids," said the President toward the end of his visit to the Lizzie Borden facility in Massachussetts.

"Noooo! Please don't go!" cried all the orphans.

"Now, kids, you know I have to. But look—I've brought you a new tape from the GOP Fairy Tale Theatre collection."

Morgan, the leader of the girls' division, got up to accept the gift. "Wow! Thank you, Uncle Newt. We've been waiting for this one—'The Boy Who Cried Wolf' with Ralph Nader."

"We really liked the one you brought last time," said Samantha.

"Oh yes," said the President. "Ronald Reagan as 'Sleeping Beauty'. You kids have been so great. I can't tear myself away. How about one last story?"

"Yaaaaaaaaay!"

RUMPEL-STEPHANOPOULOS

here once was a good little Republican girl, whose father's tobacco company had been driven out of business by high taxes and smoke-free environments. She was a very beautiful, enterprising girl, who had studied business at Kennesaw State College and built her very own matchbook advertising empire. But the little match girl's business went the way of her father's— she could not sell any matches because there was no longer anything to light that wasn't dangerous or polluting.

One day the girl's father, reduced to desperation by grinding poverty but determined not to accept charity of any kind, went to Washington. He told the ruler of the liberal government that his daughter, through her creative accounting skills, was able to turn workers' salaries directly into taxes to support the bloated welfare state.

Now the liberal government was very fond of taking money that upstanding, hard-working people had earned through honest toil, and using it to subsidize lazy bums, whiners, illegal immigrants, pornographic artists, abortionists, homosexuals, and subversives of every stripe. Government could never be big enough, and there were never enough perks to go around.

So the liberal leader ordered the girl to be brought before him. He locked her in a room filled from floor to ceiling with paychecks and said that by the time the sun rose the next morning she must turn them into 1040 forms that were all in the 100 percent tax bracket, if not more.

The little Republican girl cried and cried because she could not do any such thing. Then suddenly the door flew open and in capered a handsome young press secretary with a presidential seal emblazoned on his chest and microphones dangling from the tassles on his cap.

"Hello, dear young lady, why do you weep?"

The girl said that she must turn these paychecks into paperwork by dawn but that she did not know how.

"I can put a new spin on anything," said the curious young press secretary. "What will you give me if I do the task for you?"

"I will give you my cable subscription, complete with C-SPAN, and I will stop being an informed citizen forever."

So the press secretary burrowed busily into the pile, and by morning the job was done.

When the liberal leader came and saw the new riches that had been created for his Treasury, he was very pleased. But social welfare programs always lead to more social welfare programs, and one new tax begets another, so he shut the girl up the next night in an even larger room filled with more paychecks.

The little Republican girl cried and cried again, because she could not do any such thing. And once more the door flew open and in capered the handsome young press secretary.

"What will you give me if I do the task for you?" asked the curious man.

"I will give you my complete videotaped set of Rush Limbaugh's programs. I will never watch Rush again and will uncritically accept everything the administration tells me."

So the press secretary burrowed busily into the pile, and by morning the job was all done.

The liberal leader was delighted to see so much new revenue, enough to create a new government agency that would provide free electronic games and foreign automobiles for people on welfare. But he still was not satisfied, and he led the girl to the very largest room in the White House. "All this must be turned into tax forms tonight," he said. "And if you succeed, you shall be my mistress."

As soon as the girl was alone the press secretary came in and said, "What will you give me this time if I do the job for you?"

"I have nothing left," she moaned.

"Then promise me," said the press secretary, "that you will give me the first child born to you and the leader so that I can use it in medical experimentation at NIH."

The girl had no choice, so she promised. Secretly she

thought it was a very safe promise, because her strong family values had made her vow that she would never have sex until she married her high school sweetheart.

So once again the press secretary turned the paychecks into IRS paperwork. When the liberal leader arrived in the morning, he was delighted to find enough money to create two new federal agencies—one that would fund solar energy research in government-subsidized coal mines, and another to pay for fancy clothes, cosmetics, and baby-sitting services for welfare recipients who couldn't get a date on Saturday night.

That very night the liberal leader took the girl to a party at Senator Kennedy's house, and once she set foot on the slippery moral slope of liberalism, she wound up pregnant.

After the baby was born, the girl was very happy for a time in spite of herself. As an unemployed unwed mother the liberal government showered her with riches, which tempted her in spite of her strict moral values. But one day the curious little press secretary came to her federally subsidized Georgetown mansion and reminded her of the promise she had made. The girl loved her young child, and she offered the press secretary anything in return—her Jaguar, her opera subscription, a position as guest host on her PBS nature series. Finally her tears softened his heart. "I will give you three days," the press secretary said. "If at the end of that time you can tell me my name, I will let you keep your child."

The girl stayed awake all night thinking of all the names

she possibly could. She sent e-mail messages to every bulletin board in the land hoping to discover yet other names. The next day the press secretary came and she began reciting: Baucus, Feinstein, Bradley, Glenn, Bumpers, Heflin, Byrd, Inouye, Biden, Lautenberg, Moynihan, Pryor, Nunn, Robb, Rockefeller, Simon. . . . But to all of the names the press secretary said, "No, that is not my name."

On the second day the press secretary came again, and once more the poor girl began to recite: Abercrombie, Ackerman, Andrews, Baesler, Baldacci, Barcia, Barrett, Becerra, Beilenson, Bentsen, Berman, Bevill, Bishop, Bonior, Borski . . . on and on and on and on. But to each name the press secretary simply said, "No, that is not my name."

Just before the third day dawned the poor Republican girl was surfing the Internet when a mysterious e-mail message arrived for her with the return address nixon@prcs.dcd: "As I paced the town last night I saw a strange little man dancing around the base of the Washington Monument. And as he danced he sang:

The babe is mine, just wait and see,

She can't keep him away from me.

She'll try and try, but never guess

My name's Rumpel-Stephanopoulos!"

The girl was delighted. A little later the press secretary arrived and gleefully said, "All right now, this is your last chance. Can you tell me my name?"

"Is it George McGovern?"

"No, that is not my name!"

"Is it Adlai Stevenson?"

"No, that is not my name!"

"Is it Rumpel-Stephanopoulos?"

"Ah! How did you know? How did you know? Who leaked that information? Deep Throat strikes again!" And the press secretary stamped away in a towering rage and was never seen again.

When visiting the orphanages, the President is often accompanied by a huge entourage, including reporters, Secret Service agents, and his special undercover orphan bodyguard brigade. Landing strips have been built to accommodate Air Force One at each of the orphanage sites.

Uncle Newt's exits have become legendary. Thanks to his White House special effects staff, even his departures are a celebration of American ingenuity. To pry himself away from the grateful throngs of tykes, he carries candy and lottery tickets that he strews throughout the crowd. Then, after a hearty wave at the top of the steps, he enters Air Force One, which disappears in a huge neon-colored cloud only seconds later.

His visits touch his heart. He especially loves hearing the cheer that goes up as the orphans see the beautiful spectacle of his plane disappearing in a brilliant flash.

"Poor kids," Uncle Newt often says as he looks down toward the crowd of orphans getting smaller and smaller. "They don't know it's all done with smoke and mirrors."